The Road Between Fire and Sea

The Alchemy of Fire and Water

I0617068

For permissions or inquiries, contact: dominiqueever6@gmail.com

The Road Between Fire and Sea First Edition

ISBN: 979-8-9989014-1-6 (paperback)
ISBN: 979-8-9989014-0-9 (ebook)

Cover and design by Dominique
Printed in the United States of America

The Hero's Journey

Descent. Fire. Ocean. Becoming.

To Tía Alicia

You didn't just let me in—
you welcomed every piece of me.
Thank you for opening your home and your heart.

To Randy

It wasn't just a place to live.
It was healing. It was safety.
It was years I'll never forget.
Thank you for being part of that.

And to the ones who held me when the fire came—
You were part of the rebuild.
Thank you for holding space
when everything else fell away.

For Malibu, my soul dog, who found me by the
sea and carried me through the flames.

For Malibu, the place that held both my love and loss.

For every soul touched by wildfire, and for those who
have learned that when the world falls away, the only
true home is the one you build inside yourself.

Table of Contents

Preface

This book was born in the aftermath—
in the silence that follows loss,
in the smoke that clings after the fire,
in the salt that stays when the sea has gone.

I didn't write these poems to be understood.
I wrote them to survive.

To remember what burned.
To honor what stayed.
To find language for the things that almost broke me,
and the beauty that bloomed anyway.

These pages carry the scent of ash,
the rhythm of waves,
and the ache of things that couldn't be saved.

They are for anyone who has stood barefoot in ruin
and still dared to hope.

If you are holding this book,
then some part of you already knows:

Grief is a teacher.
Fire is an altar.
And healing is not a return—
it is a becoming.

CHAPTER I

Sanctuary Before the Burn

There was a time I called it safe—
before the smoke curled beneath the door,
before I knew that even sanctuaries can catch fire.

1

The Village

My Tía built a home in the Palisades—
with my cousin's hands,
with holy resilience,
passed down like recipes,
with Mexican love that lingered in every room.

She called me Mejía,
like it meant something sacred,
something strong.

There were gatherings that spilled into the night,
Christmas Eve filled with light and tradition,
dancing in the kitchen,
smoking outside beneath the stars.

Spanish prayers lived in the air,
meals that healed beyond hunger,
and stories that wove through generations.

Children walked to school,
church bells rang,
and the village moved
with faith,
with family,
with fire.

If it weren't for her,
I'd have never found this place—
never known that home
could begin with a name
and grow into everything.

Author's Note:

Before there was Malibu, there was this quiet beginning.

Malibu, My Saint

My soul dog,
found on the grounds that healed me.
No collar,
only instinct and presence,
climbing Las Flores like she'd always belonged.

It was All Saints' Day—
the canyon quiet,
as if it knew
a saint had arrived.

You came after loss,
but you didn't fill an absence—
you opened something new.
A beginning wrapped in fur,
in stillness,
in choosing me
before I could choose myself.

You were more than a dog.
You were the spirit of the land,
the breath of memory,
the proof that healing walks beside us
when we least expect it.

Eyes Before Words

It wasn't sudden.
It was soft—
like I had always known your eyes
before I'd ever seen your face.

You looked at me
in my doorway,
like you found something
you weren't sure existed.

And I looked back
like I'd been waiting
to be found.

We didn't need words.
The silence between us
was already speaking
louder than we ever could.

CHAPTER II

The Descent

It didn't all fall at once.
First, the silence changed shape.
Then the light turned strange.
And something I thought I could hold—slipped.

The Unraveling (Night)

Franklin came in the dark of night.
Ash fell like snow,
and the hills caught fire.
My sister and I—silent—
watched the glow grow higher.

When the power went,
we lit candles instead—
surrounded by fear
and what's next,
with her by my side,
her hand in mine.

Banging doors,
empty roads,
a warning we tried to ignore.

The moon—so white but surrounded by red—
has seen this all before.
She knew it long before we did.

The winds—out of our control—
she speaks in escape.

The Unraveling (Morning)

We watched the haunting sun rise in confusion,
surrounded by candles and illusions.

We left with the aching sun,
smoke in our waves,
PCH stripped bare—
a month before
we lost it all there.

The Moment The Veil Thinned

The brass didn't break that morning.
It lifted—
low, reverent,
like it was praying in a language
older than words.

New Orleans was alive.
But the veil was thin.
And I felt it—
in the way the joy trembled,
in the hush beneath the horns.

I walked beside him,
feet on Bourbon Street,
where sound and spirit
never quite stay separate.

I think of that night often.
The color.
The motion.
The music that knew
what none of us did yet.

And I think of the next morning—
the stillness,
the names,
suddenly gone.

I think of the fragility of life,
how breath is borrowed,
how joy walks hand in hand with risk.

I've seen how easily it can vanish.
I've felt how sacred it is to stay.

They don't know what I carry.
But the city did.
The music did.
And in that thin space,
so did I.

The veil never breaks.
it only lifts for those who listen.

Author's Note:

I wrote this just days before the fire.
A premonition I didn't yet understand—
the smoke arrived,
but the words came first.

Fragments In The Smoke

They think they know me,
but I am only fragments to them—
a fleeting figure in the smoke,
a name whispered but never understood,
a presence that dissolves when they try to hold it.

Even those who hold me closest
see only what I let them,
blind to the depth beneath the surface.
Not even those who created me
have truly seen me.

They look at me as if I am whole,
but they cannot see the fractures I carry,
the weight buried beneath every escape,
the complexity that I have hidden
where no one dares to look.

I say I want to be seen,
not to be known.
To be known is to be unraveled,
to be claimed by eyes that will never understand.

But to be seen—
to flicker briefly in their awareness,
a shadow they cannot hold—
that is freedom.

I've drifted through their lives,
invisible and infinite,
unclaimed and untethered.

To be unknown, even to myself,
is to belong to nothing,
and in that nothingness, I am free.

But I bear it all—the ash and the absence,
the echoes of streets walked too close to disaster.

I've lived a life that moves through flames
without ever being consumed,

but the fire has followed me for too long.
I am done running.

The smoke calls my name now,
its pull as steady as my breath,
and I will not turn away.
The fire waits,
and this time,
I am ready to go.

Echoes of a Wildfire

You followed me across the ages,
etched our names
into the heart of your masterpiece.

I lay here now, lost in thought,
no longer able to outrun myself.

The parallels haunt me, the leaking clouds suffocate me,
this pull—this gravity of you—is too much.

You were always above me, always ahead,
and then, in an instant, everything we knew disappeared.

Days before, I burned down the walls of my heart,
tore them apart to let you in,
only to be left with words unsaid,
love unspoken, truths abandoned.

Then the fire came, and it wasn't just the
world that turned to ashes—
it was us.

You lost every chance you had.
You stood there, watching me vanish into specks of dust,
assuming I'd always remain, always orbit around you.

But everything I was burned away,
left in the rubble of what you could've held.

Your chance is gone now,
gone like the love that was a wildfire,
burning too fiercely, too carelessly,
until nothing was left.

We lost everything to the flames.
But I, I became your greatest loss.

The dust will never settle for you,
because you'll never forget me.

Not as the one who was lost,
but as the phoenix that rose,
brighter than the fire,
beyond the ashes you left me in.

Before

This is the place we'll always call before,
Where the earth cradled my tears,
Pulled me from my roots,
And gave me my soul dog,
Her name bound to this sacred ground—Malibu.

She is gone,
And now, so are you.
The light, once golden,
The sunshine, once warm,
The waves, once whispering wisdom,
Now thick with ash,
Muted in grief.

I loved you in the before,
And now, you bring only togetherness—
A strange, hollow unity.

Together,
We will hold this void.

Invocation:
The One Who Waited

For the girl who waited
without proof.
Without rescue.
Without sound.

For the girl who held my name
beneath the silence.

I cry for her now.
And she knows I made it.

She became the ocean waiting at the end of the fire.

CHAPTER III

Alchemy of Elements

What the fire couldn't burn,
the sea carried away.

She spoke in phases, never in full.

Cosmic Scripts

I won't play the Sun's role—
for I am the moon:
a celestial soul.

Stars dangle from my ears—
tales untold,
mystery of the darkest night made new.

Her crescent's curve—
lost in you.
Sensual,
strange,
a captivating view.

Blood-stained moon:
my subconscious mind.

Waning gibbous on a Tuesday—
a bit unaligned.
Distinct and unique,
a lunar spree,
no desire to change—
just let it be.

Meet me where sanity intertwines.
Will you fathom my truth
through my phases?

Someday,
in full glow,
our paths will align.

But tonight—
waxing gibbous confines.

The Road Between
Fire And Sea

We once lived along the road
caught between fire and sea.

You closed yourself inside your cage.
I walked away without leaving a trace.

That is the difference between us.

You carved my name into your hat—
I never asked.

I saw the flame go from red to blue.
I saw your cage collapse into quiet dust.

I saw your hat burn,
and my name you carved rise with the smoke,
disappearing into a place
you'll never reach.

Canyon of Green
—By the Sea

Dust collecting beside my bed—
a shattered archive of thoughts and dreams.
I've only ever known
a life trapped inside my head.

What a way to live—
moving blindly through the unknown,
day by day,
unchanged,
though yesterday always slips out of reach.

Dissociated by dawn,
lost in a wonderland
that nearly drowns by dusk.

Crocodile eyes of green—
not out of sight,
but maybe out of spite.

I am a delicate creature,
spinning in the night,
dwelling in a world
you may never truly see.

It is not what it seems.

But if you ever need to find me,
look to the sea—
where my feet bleed for all that is me
in the canyon of green
by the sea.

Sixteen Was Taken

Stripped of home,
of rhythm,
of freedom.

Twenty-eight stood barefoot
Watching it all burn—
but this time,
I was the one who let go.

Grief wore many faces.
At nineteen, it looked like him.

The Immaculate Misconception

Today, the truth whispers to me—
a hazed mirage of glass
stained on my bed of rage and sage.
Bruised is my wall
from the pain you caused.
She was only a teen.
You were nearly thirty.

You dragged an impeccable transformation
into a state of impuration and suffocation

—

from the lake of fire
to damnation.

I watched my flowers rise
only to taste their death
on one too many occasions.

You walked down the aisle of lies,
The Last Supper tattooed on his chest,
Treated me unholy—
But weren't you the one who exploited me?
In a matter of weeks, I lost a part of me—
walking down the hallway of white
with empty arms,
and gone went my mind.

A vision of light turned to black.
The conception of us
was never immaculate—
just tragic.

I pray your daughter never endures
what I once did
from your kind.
What did you expect of me—
to have it all figured out
at nineteen?

Oh, how suddenly I see—
you were leeching off me.
Oh, how long it took the truth to speak.
And now—I'm living out my dreams.
Oh, how I wish
I could've told you that
at twenty.

And I Cried.

for the girl taken at sixteen.

Not because I missed her—
but because she finally looked back at me.

Barefoot in the aftermath,
we wept like the sea,
and I let her go.

And at the end of the fire
—she was already water.

She was the fire.
She was the flood.
She was always me.

The fire burned away the illusion.
The sea softened the wound.
Now the mirror clears—
And I begin to see myself

My Reflection Spills

I watched faces melt from my life,
into the soil where my roots first broke.
It was always me who left—
never out of malice,
only translucence.

My spirit lingers in your coffee,
a soft ghost
screaming beneath the surface.
How does it feel
to lose me for the final time?

She still speaks my name, like we're paused,
waiting for my sweet return.
I still haunt him in his dreams,
though he holds her like she might become me.

—

They all pose like their life depends on it,
but they still feel me
in the spaces between smiles and voids.

I outgrew the smallness
they tried to keep me in.
They chose comfort over connection—
a girl they could name—
instead of one who could unmask them.

Still, I return—
not to stay,
but to reclaim the girl I left behind.

This time, the waves told the truth.

You loved me for years—
and still do.
But never in the light.
And I—
I was born for the moon.

Now, deep in the tabernacle of my heart,
I know—
you sure as hell aren't for me.

I close the curtain
on the place that mistook performance for peace.

Where the county glowed with orange light—
artificially flavored,
...but nothing ever tasted real.

CHAPTER IV

The Path Backward,
The Pull Forward

The Week They
Couldn't Follow

I crossed something that week.
A line they didn't see,
between the version of me who hoped for softness,
and the one who knows she is the softness—
even after the smoke.

They saw news alerts.
I saw the veil.

They saw my apartment burn.
I saw the blueprint of my next life.

They saw survival.
I lived ceremony.

I don't blame them for not following.
It wasn't their fire.

But I carry it now.
Gently.
Glowing.

And if they ever ask—
I'll tell them:
There are wildflowers now.
Right where the walls used to be.

The Return Was
Never For You

Just because I returned to my roots does
not mean they called me home.
He wants me to stay, but I did not return to be kept.

After all these years away—
you should know I was never yours to keep.

I return to remember
what I am meant to leave behind.

And I leave without weight.

Sometimes return is just the
final rite of departure.

There are places you must leave to remember
who you are. This is a farewell to the illusion
of belonging where I never truly did.

May this reflection spill into your own becoming.

Two Realms

It's pretty wild,
to live in two completely different realms—
simultaneously.

One hand holds ashes—
the remnants of homes,
stories scorched but spirits unburnt.
They rise,
offering love in smoke-wrapped prayers,
still choosing gratitude
when there's barely anything left to hold.

The other?
In the comfort of their own bed,
Dripping in abundance,
yet drowning in complaint.
Every small inconvenience
a tragedy.
Every mirror, a portal to pity.
The weight of the mundane
breaking backs that never carried real loss.

I hope their illusions collapse.
I hope the veil tears just enough
for them to see—
really see.

But maybe they won't.

Maybe their lives will move in loops,
untouched by the fire,
never shifted by winds of change,
never cracked open
to the beauty beneath broken things.

Because not everything is what it seems.
And gratitude—
that's literally it.
The truth wrapped in simplicity,
the anchor in chaos,
the portal between realms.

Grocery Store Apparition

The blood orange glows like artificial moons,
stacked in rows too perfect to be touched.
Everything hums—
refrigerators, overhead lights,
the breath of strangers who pretend not to see each other.

I trail behind my body.
She moves like she knows what she's doing—
but I'm watching from somewhere above aisle 7,
floating above the rows of metallic amnesia,
wondering when we became two.

A child screams in the distance.
It echoes like a fire alarm underwater.
No one flinches.
This is normal here.
The sound of innocence being silenced by routine.

I stare too long at a loaf of bread,
its plastic skin tight like hospital wrap.
The expiration date feels prophetic.
I put it back. I take it again.
The world tilts slightly.

Somewhere near the crackers
I remember being small
and trying to put my hand through the TV—
not to reach anything,
but to escape.

Sometimes I still feel the screen hum inside me.

Someone bumps my shoulder and I vanish.
Not completely—just enough.
Just enough to forget what I needed
or why I ever came.

A man is laughing near the wine.

His voice spills red across the linoleum.
I want to ask him what it's like to be that solid.
To move through aisles and never dissolve.

At checkout, I smile with the wrong mouth.
Hands trembling, heart absent.
I say "thank you" like a ghost rehearsing civility.
They bag my groceries. I bag my dissociation.

Outside, the sun is blinding.
But I still feel fluorescent.

CHAPTER V

Thresholds of Becoming

We Were Dreamland

Malibu Barbie was framed on the wall,
watching over us like a pink-lipped oracle—
sun-blonde, unbothered,
a flash of girlhood turned myth,
still holding her throne in plastic and power.

Polaroids circled her like stars—
us laughing in the kitchen,
wrapped in towels,
barefoot and burning with joy
that felt both timeless and brand new.

The apartment was built in the 1950s,
but it pulsed with our presence.
We danced like the walls were listening,
like the floor had a heartbeat,
like time had folded to make room for us.

I still have flashbacks
of every corner—
every mirror,
every shadow,
every time we remembered
who we were before the world tried to tell us.

In the middle of the night,
the pink-tiled shower held our voices,
mermaid songs rising with steam,
blessing the chaos with shimmer and salt.

We didn't perform.
We didn't shrink.

And we weren't visiting dreamland.

We were dreamland—
On PCH,
in memory.
in sisterhood.
The magic.
The becoming.

We were mythology in lipstick and pink tile—
not made up, just misunderstood.

We baptized our girlhood in glitter and grief.

The Threshold

I am not where I was.
But I am not yet where I am going.

This is the space between versions—
a lunar pause between her phases.
The glimmer of something
not quite dissolved,
not yet born.

I keep finding pieces of myself
in unexpected places—
in places I dreamed before I lived them,
in faces I almost remembered,
in the sudden ache
of outgrowing what I once prayed for.

This is not an ending.
It's a doorway.
And though I move slowly,
I move with an inner knowing—
forged in the quietest parts of me.

Of a life I once only sensed,
now sparkling above the horizon,
arriving slowly,
like I always knew it would.

Because becoming requires a certain kind of grief.
And freedom
asks us to say goodbye
to what we loved
but could not carry forward.

I am not lost.
I'm just arriving—
from a thousand different directions.

Arrival

I didn't even notice it at first—
the way I began to take up space again,
not with noise,
but with presence.

The ache didn't vanish.
But it softened.
And beneath it,
something rooted.

I woke up one morning
and didn't miss
who I used to be.
Didn't long for what I'd left.
Only breathed
deeper.

This is not a rebirth.
This is a remembering.
Not a new self—
but the true one,
finally given room to rise.

There is peace now,
not because it's easy,
but because it's mine.

And every version of me
that broke,
that loved,
that danced barefoot in dreamland—
she's still here.

But now,
so am I.

CHAPTER VI

The Bloom

Rise

If you ever feel lost again,
read this.

Remember the girl
who fell and stood again,
the woman who bled beauty
into every fracture.

You are not starting over.
You are continuing
a legacy of rising.

Bloom

I bloomed
when no one was watching—
in solitude.
in the dark.

Right beside where I used to reside,
The wildflowers rose.
So did I.

No waiting.
No need to be seen.

The bloom was always me.

Peace is the Loudest Thing I've Ever Known

Not silence.
Peace.
The kind that doesn't ache.
The kind that doesn't wait.
The kind that says—
I am here.
I am whole.
I am not missing anything.

The Mirror's Choice

This morning, the mirror stared deeper than skin,
a battlefield blooming beneath my reflection.
I saw two paths—
one paved in pity,
one burning in purpose.

The voices inside whispered heavy doubts,
ghosts of every almost, every could-have-been.
They tempted me:
"Fold into the hurt,"
"Wear the weight like a crown."
But something stronger stirred.

Today, I will not worship my wounds.
Today, I won't bow to the version of me
that settles for silence and sighs.
Today, I lace up the shoes of my wildest dreams
and run headfirst into the fire I built.

It's time—
to craft the life I once only tasted in daydreams,
to paint with every color fear told me to hide,
to finally live like my soul has been begging me to.

The mirror doesn't lie—
but today, I get to decide who answers back.

Author's Closing Note:

This was never just about reflection—
it was about return.
To the self I buried,
the voice I softened,
the fire I feared.

If you made it here,
may you choose the mirror, too.
And may the answer that looks back
be one born not of survival,
but of becoming.

www.ingramcontent.com/pod-product-compliance
Lightning Source LLC
Chambersburg PA
CBHW040857120626
46551CB00001B/62

* 9 7 9 8 9 9 8 9 0 1 4 1 6 *